It's Easy - I don't need my thumb

By Mary Fern

It's easy - I don't need my thumb

It won't make me sad or glum – I don't need my thumb

I can do it –
Thumbs away
today!

We are going to tell you a secret that we bet you didn't know!

A Dream
Dragon visits
every night.
While you and I
are sleeping
tight.

There are five Dream Dragons and I'll tell you thier names

Darren

Dart

Swooper

Dylan

Dash

Dylan the Dragon is his name. And brilliant dreams are his game.

When Dylan sees
your happy smile.
His magic will make
your dreams
worthwhile.

Dylan swishes
his magic tail.
Soon you'll find
yourself in
dreamland.

Wonderful dreams
will fill your head.
While you sleep
snugly in your bed.

Dylan just needs to see your wonderful smile.
So tonight don't suck your thumb for a while.

It won't make
you sad or glum –
You don't need
your thumb

So when Dylan or
one of his friends
call tonight.
Make sure your
smile is shining
bright.

It won't make
you sad or glum –
You don't need
your thumb

You might dream you are in a castle and you are the King. With dragons and horses and other wonderful things.

Maybe you'll be a pirate with treasure on an island. Hidden in secret deep in the sand.

It won't make
you sad or glum –
You don't need
your thumb

Maybe you'll dream of a spaceman in his ship. Past planets and stars he'll zip.

Just remeber it
won't make you
sad or glum -
You don't need
your thumb

Or at the seaside with
your bucket and spade.
Lots of hard work
there are sandcastles
to be made.

Happy Dreams

The End

Part of the
Mary Fern
Children's
Series - also
available on
audible

Printed in Great Britain
by Amazon

23032380R00016